The Hard Thing About Hard Things

Building a Business When There Are No Easy Answers

by

Ben Horowitz

A 30-MINUTE INSTAREAD SUMMARY

Please Note:

This is an unofficial summary. We encourage you to purchase the full-form book before or after reading the summary.

Book Overview

Ben Horowitz is the author and narrative of this bestselling book. Ben describes being the grandchild of Communist grandparents and the child of a father who was indoctrinated in Communist philosophy. He remembers being a quiet and shy child, afraid of almost everything and everyone around him. As he grew up, he learned about the world around him experience by experience. As a young boy, he learned that facing his fears could lead to great discoveries. He realized in high school that looking at the same situation from several differing perspectives would totally alter their outcomes. In college, he learned that first impressions (both given and received) are not always accurate and that only true knowledge is reliable and powerful. These life lessons prepared him for one of the biggest challenges of his life: starting his own business.

Ben started his career as an engineer in the Silicon Valley. He switched jobs a few times, and learned many valuable lessons by doing so. One of the biggest things he learned was that it is crucial for company founders to run their own companies. Ben went on to become co-founder of the first cloud-based service, Loudcloud. He uses his own experiences to illustrate the challenges that arise when attempting to start, run, and sell a technology business. In addition to sharing his stories, Ben analyzes the problems that affected him and his partners and shares the insights he has gained along the way. He addresses the difficulties in securing funding, becoming and remaining competitive, hiring and retaining top-notch employees, and being an effective CEO. He also delves into the specifics for dealing with common difficulties once your business is up and running. He gives practical advice for demoting a loyal colleague or friend. He also discusses the value of using titles and promotions and how to make sure you don't create or promote politics within your organization when doing so. Tips are provided for how to manage stress and stay sane when hundreds of people are counting on you not only for a paycheck, but also to successfully run the company. He highlights the importance of honest, straightforward communication explaining the importance of conveying not only the goals, but also the current reality to everyone involved in the business. Ben also provides insights about hiring, including the fact that intelligent people don't always make the best employees.

Finally Ben discusses how to make decisions regarding selling your company and just how to do it when you decide you want or need to sell. In the end, Ben reflects about how he felt after he sold his company and wound up working for Hewlett Packard as head of the software business. He thought not only about his future, but his past, wondering if others had the same difficulties as he had experienced starting their own businesses. He wondered why they didn't write anything down about what they'd learned. He wondered also why very few startup advisers and venture capitalists had little experience starting companies. Then he sent a message to his friend and colleague, Marc Andreessen about starting a venture capital firm. Ben went on to co-found the wildly successful Andreessen Horowitz venture capital firm and become a popular author of his blog and this book.

List of Characters

Ben: Entrepreneur and author, narrator of the book

Cartheu: Ben's brother-in-law who often gives him advice

Felicia: Ben's wife

John: Ben's father-in-law

Marc Andreessen: Mosaic inventor, co-founder of Netscape, co-founder of Loudcloud, and Ben's current partner at the venture capital firm, Andreessen Horowitz

Jim Clark: Founder of Silicon Graphics, co-founder of Netscape, and Ben's business partner

Dr. Timothy Howes: Co-inventor of the Lightweight Directory Access Protocol and co-founder of Loudcloud

In Sik Rhee: Co-founder of Loudcloud

Bill Campbell: Ben's friend and a Loudcloud board member

Introduction

Ben explains that every time he reads a self-help or management book, he thinks about the fact that it didn't really address the hard things like laying people off or having good people start demanding unreasonable things. The problem with self-help books is that they try to provide a recipe for dealing with difficult, dynamic situations. Challenging situations can not be solved with a formula. Instead of using a formula in this book, the author presents his story as he progressed from an entrepreneur to CEO to venture capitalist. He shares some of the lessons he has learned along the way. He explains that although circumstances may differ, patterns and lessons resonate with each experience. For the last several years, he has shared lessons learned on his popular blog. Many people have emailed him to ask about the stories behind the lessons. Ben shares that he has been inspired along the way by many family members, friends, and advisers who have helped him. Hip-hop/rap music has also inspired him because these artists aspire to be both great and successful. He also admires that rappers see themselves as entrepreneurs.

1: From Communist to Venture Capitalist

Ben's grandparents were card-carrying Communists. His dad grew up indoctrinated in the Communist philosophy. Ben's family moved to Berkeley, California, in 1968. His dad then became the editor of the famous New Left magazine, *Ramparts*. When Ben was five, his family moved to Bonita Avenue, a middle-class Berkeley neighborhood. One day, a friend of Ben's older brother, Roger, pointed to an African American kid down the block who happened to be riding in a red wagon. Roger dared Ben to go tell the kid to give him his wagon, and if he refused, to spit in his face and call him a racial epithet. Roger wasn't a racist and did not come from a bad family. Ben later found out that he had schizophrenia. He had wanted to see a fight. Ben was afraid of Roger, and his demand put him in a very tough situation. He thought Roger would beat him up if he didn't do what he told him to do. He was also afraid to ask for the wagon. He walked toward the boy and when he got near enough, he said, "Can I ride in your wagon?" The boy, Joel Clark Jr., said, "Sure." Ben turned to look at Roger and saw that he was gone. Ben went on to play with Joel all day, and they have been best friends ever since. That experience taught Ben that being scared didn't mean he was gutless. He learned that what he did mattered and determined whether he would be a hero or a coward. If he had completely followed Roger's order, he would have never met his best friend. He also learned not to judge things by appearance alone. If a person does not make the effort to get to know someone or something, that person really knows nothing. According to Ben, shortcuts to knowledge do not exist. He also believes that conventional wisdom is not always the best, and sometimes following it can be worse than knowing nothing at all.

Ben worked hard over the years to avoid being influenced by first impressions and blindly following conventions. He joined the Berkeley High School football team with no prior experience in the sport. Since Ben was the only player on the team who also excelled academically, he had several different social circles. This was great for him because he got to hang out with lots of different kids that had different views. He was surprised to learn that a diverse perspective changed the meaning of every important event in the world. When Run-D.M.C.'s *Hard Times* album came out, the football team was excited, but nobody in his calculus class said a word about it. Looking at the world through such different lenses helped him learn how to separate facts from perceptions. This was a skill that helped him immensely when he became an entrepreneur and CEO. In difficult situations, when the facts seemed to demand a particular outcome, he learned to look for different narratives and explanations from different perspectives to inform him. The existence of an alternate scenario is usually what is needed to keep hope alive in a troubled workforce.

One summer while he was in college, Ben got a job as an engineer at Silicon Graphics. He loved the company and thought he wanted to work there for the rest of his life. After he finished graduate school, he went back to work for SGI. After working there for a year, he met the former head of marketing for the company, Roselie Buonauro. Roselie recruited him, and he went to work for her at a startup called NetLabs. This turned out to be a very bad decision. Roselie and her husband were brought in by venture capitalists as the professional management team to run the company, but they understood little about NetLab's products or technology. Ben began to recognize the importance of founders running their own companies. At this time, Ben's second daughter, Mariah, had been diagnosed with autism. Working at a startup was hard for the family because he was desperately needed at home. He quit NetLabs and found a job that would allow him more time for his family at Lotus Development.

One day while he was working at Lotus, a co-worker showed Ben a new product called Mosaic. Mosaic was a graphical interface to the Internet. Ben was amazed by it and knew it was clearly the future. He wondered why he was wasting his time working on anything but the Internet. Months later, he read about Netscape, a company co-founded by former Silicon Graphics founder Jim Clark and Mosaic inventor, Marc Andreessen. Ben decided he wanted a job there. He called a friend with connections and asked if he could get him an interview. He interviewed and got a call from the hiring manager the next day. They wanted him to interview with company co-founder, Marc Andreessen.

At the time, most people believed the Internet would only be used by scientists and researchers. Marc and Jim Clark decided that creating a more secure, more functional, and easier to use browser could make the Internet the network of the future. This became the mission of Netscape. During the interview with Marc, Ben was asked about the history of email, collaboration software, and what the future might hold. Ben was shocked by how much Marc knew at the young age of twenty-two. A week after being interviewed, Ben got the job. At Netscape, he was placed in charge of the Enterprise Web Server product line. Netscape was thriving when Microsoft announced that it was bundling its browser, Internet Explorer, with Windows 95 for free. Netscape's revenue came from browser sales, and Microsoft controlled more than 90 percent of operating systems, so this was a huge problem for Netscape. The company told its investors that they would make their money on Web servers. Ben worked with his department head, Mike Homer, to develop a comprehensive answer to the Microsoft threat. They planned to offer a cheap, open alternative to the Microsoft BackOffice product line. They acquired two companies and cut a deal with Informix, a database company, to get unlimited relational database access through the Web for just $50 a copy. They assembled the entire package, and Mike named it Netscape SuiteSpot. They lined everything up for a major launch on

March 5th, 1996, in New York. Ben was shocked two weeks before the launch to find that Marc had revealed the strategy to *Computer Reseller News*. Ben couldn't believe that Marc had ruined the launch by revealing their strategy early in his interview with CRN.

Suitespot quickly grew to a $400 million a year business. Marc and Ben have been friends and business partners ever since. The reason the relationship works so well is that they upset each other every day by finding something wrong with each other's thinking.

At the end of 1998, under immense pressure from Microsoft, Netscape was sold to America Online. Netscape had invented many of the foundational technologies of the modern Internet, including JavaScript, SSL, and Cookies. With AOL, Ben was assigned to run the e-commerce platform, and Marc was the chief technology officer. Marc and Ben realized that AOL saw itself as more of a media company than a technology company. They started talking about ideas for forming a new company and talking with potential co-founders. Timothy Howes was co-inventor of the Lightweight Directory Access Protocol. In Sik Rhee was the fourth member of their team. He had co-founded an application server company that had been acquired by Netscape. As they discussed ideas, In Sik complained that when they tried to connect an AOL partner on the e-commerce platform, the partner's site crashed because it couldn't handle the traffic load. Deploying software to scale to millions of users was difficult, and they figured there needed to be a company to do it well. They came up with the idea of a computing cloud that would prevent software developers from having to worry about security, scaling, and disaster recovery. In 1999, the team incorporated their new company, Loudcloud.

Key Takeaways

- Fear can lead to new opportunities if faced properly.
- Diversity and looking at things from different perspectives opens doors.
- Challenging each other's thinking creates great friendships and successful business partnerships.

2: "I Will Survive"

Marc and Ben found Andy Rachleff, a venture capitalist from Benchmark Capital, to work with. Benchmark agreed to invest $15 million at a pre-money valuation of $45 million. Marc would also invest $6 million and serve as the chairman of the board. Tim Howes would be chief technology officer, and Ben would serve as CEO. Andy advised Ben to think about how he had run the company if the capital were free. After just four months in business, they raised an additional $45 million from Morgan Stanley with no covenants and no payments for three years. Ben took Andy's advice and ran with it. They built the infrastructure and signed up customers at a rapid rate. After seven months, they had booked $10 million in contracts. They were in a race against the competition and needed to find quality people. They began hiring thirty employees a month. By the next quarter, they booked $27 million worth of new contracts. Then the dot-com crash on March 10th, 2000, occurred. Startups lost value, investors lost wealth, and dot-coms went out of business overnight. The team now needed to raise even more money because their $66 million in equity and debt had already been used. Because of the dot-com crash, raising money was much harder. Ben had nearly three hundred employees and very little cash left. It was during this time that he learned the most important rule of raising money privately: Look for a market of one because you only need one investor to say "yes." This mindset allowed him to ignore the investors that said "no" and keep searching instead of becoming discouraged and giving up.

The team eventually found investors and raised $120 million. The sales forecast for the quarter was $100 million, and Ben thought things might be okay. He hoped to migrate their customer base away from dot-com bombs to traditional customers such as Nike, their largest customer at that time. They finished the third quarter of 2000 with $37 million in bookings rather than $100 million.

Ben needed to raise money again but nobody was willing to invest. They had gone from being the hottest startup in the Valley to un-fundable in just six months. Ben had 477 employees. He decided they should consider going public as that seemed to be the only option left to raise money. He prepared a list of pros and cons of an Initial Public Offering (IPO). He knew that LoudCloud board member Bill Campbell would be the hardest person to persuade, but he was able to do it. With Bill's support, Ben convinced the board that they needed to go public. They had negative press heading into the IPO because they were said to be too reliant on dot-coms and had lost millions of dollars over the last 12 months. They decided to offer at $10 per share after an upcoming reverse split that would value the company at just under $700 million. Ben called an all-company meeting to announce that they were going to try to go public, and that they would have to reverse split the stock two for one. Each employee owned a certain percentage of the company, and when things were going well, employees had heard stories of a potential $100 per share stock price. Many had calculated their fantasy price per share. Ben's announcement immediately cut their fantasy numbers in half because of the reverse split. His employees were furious. He went on a three-week road show. The Loudcloud offering finally sold at $6 a share, and they raised $162.5 million.

As they entered their first quarter as a public company, customers became anxious, the macroeconomic environment worsened, and sales prospects dropped. Ben reviewed the numbers and found that they would meet their forecast for the quarter, but not for the year. They slashed their original forecast of $75 million in projected revenue to $55 million. Ben then had to lay off 15 percent of their employees. Goldman Sachs and Morgan Stanley both dropped research coverage meaning their analysts would no longer follow the company's progress on behalf of their clients. The stock price dropped from $6 to $2 per share.

 The company soldiered on and had a strong third quarter. Then September 11th threw the world into chaos. Ben knew the company was in a very fragile state, and he needed to do something. He asked himself what the worst thing that could happen was, and the answer was always the same: they would go bankrupt. One day, he asked himself a different question, "What would I do if we went bankrupt?" He'd buy their software, Opsware, which ran in Loudcloud, out of bankruptcy and start a software company. He then asked himself if there was a way to do that without going bankrupt. Ben immediately assigned a team of ten engineers to begin the process of separating Opsware from Loudcloud. They called the project "Oxide".

Loudcloud beat their target for the year with $57 million in revenue against their $55 million forecast. Their stock rose to $4 per share. They were ready to start trying to raise more money when Ben got a call from Atriax, an online foreign currency exchange and their biggest customer. The CEO of Atriax informed Ben that the company was bankrupt and could not pay any of the $25 million they owed Loudcloud. Ben knew Loudcloud was doomed, and he had to launch "Oxide". What made matters worse was the fact that 440 of the 450 employees worked in the cloud business, so Ben couldn't even tell his executive team what he was considering doing. He knew he could trust John O'Farrell who ran business and corporate development. John and Ben worked to identify companies that might be interested in buying Loudcloud. A company called EDS agreed to buy Loudcloud for $63.5 million in cash and assume its associated liabilities. Though Ben felt better, he still would need to sell 150 of his employees to EDS and lay off another 140. When he called Bill Campbell to let him know the deal was done, Bill advised him to let his employees know right away whether they were working for him, working for EDS, or looking for a job. That piece of advice was invaluable. He had to treat his people fairly, or those who stayed would never trust him again.

Key Takeaways

- Think about what you would do if money wasn't an issue; this opens the door for creative solutions.
- When looking for investors, look for a market of one because you only need one "yes".
- Treat your employees fairly and always tell them the truth.

3: This Time With Feeling

Once the EDS sale was finished, Ben felt like the company was back in good shape, but his shareholders felt differently. All of the large shareholders bailed out, and the stock price fell to $0.35 per share. Ben needed to take his remaining employees off-site to explain his Opsware plan to them. He rented hotel rooms in Santa Cruz and took his remaining eighty employees out for one night of drinking and a day of explaining the Opsware opportunity. He explained that it was a brand-new company, and that he was issuing everyone new stock grants as of that day. He asked those who were thinking about quitting to quit immediately. Only two employees quit. Next, Ben had to rebuild the executive team.

EDS agreed to a $20 million a year contract with Opsware. The Opsware deployment had too many technical issues, and EDS was very unhappy. EDS wanted to end the deployment immediately, and they wanted their money back. Ben sent Jason Rosenthal and Anthony Wright, his top two lieutenants on the account to meet with Frank Johnson who controlled the servers at EDS. Frank gave Anthony sixty days to fix all of the technical issues. It was at this time that Ben learned a valuable lesson: when a large organization attempts anything, a single person can delay the whole project. He had daily meetings scheduled with Anthony and Jason to prevent any delays. In working with Frank, Anthony found out that EDS used a product that inventoried their hardware and software from a company called Tangram. Frank loved the product, but was going to be forced to use a different product that was free. Anthony told Ben that if Tangram could be free with Opsware, Frank would love them. Ben looked into buying Tangram. He negotiated a deal to buy it for $10 million in cash and stock, then called Frank to tell him they would include all Tangram software for free as part of his Opsware contract. Frank was ecstatic. They had saved the account and the company!

Next, the company lost three new clients to a new competitor, BladeLogic. The stock price dropped back down to $2.90. Ben pulled the engineering team together and asked them to commit fully to the company for six months. He wanted them to come early and stay late. They had to strategize about their product. Innovation requires knowledge, skill and courage. Ben asked his team to completely reinvent the product. Nine months later, they had a new product that they were happy with, but Ben still asked the team the question, "What are we *not* doing? The staff agreed that the one thing they still weren't doing was automating the network. Ben had two choices; he could start a new project or buy one of the four existing network automation companies. He'd learned early in his career that all decisions were objective until the first line of code was written. After that, decisions became emotional. Ben negotiated a deal to buy Rendition Networks for $33 million. Three months after the acquisition, they negotiated a deal with Cisco Systems to resell their product. The Cisco deal paid more than 90 percent of the acquisition costs.

The software business approached a $150 million revenue run rate. Eventually, other companies started making offers to buy Opsware. Ben struggled to decide if they should sell at $11 per share. Technology and the landscape were changing so quickly with virtualization that he knew they would soon need to make major changes to the product to stay on top. He discussed the decision with some of his direct reports, and they advised him to sell. They decided they would only sell for $14 per share or more. Hewlett-Packard offered $14.25 per share or $1.65 billion in cash. Ben had spent eight years of his life to build Opsware, and was sick that it was over until he realized that selling was the smartest thing he'd ever done. He felt like his business life had ended. He had gone through every step from founding to going public, to selling, and he'd learned so much!

Key Takeaways

- When trying to outdo competitors, it is important to ask what you are *not* doing.
- After the first line of code is written, decisions are no longer objective in the technology business.

- The best way to learn to found a business, go public, and sell a business is by doing.

4: When Things Fall Apart

In the process of building a company, you must believe there is always an answer, and you can't pay attention to the odds of finding that answer. There is no secret to being a successful CEO; however, the ability to focus and make the best move when there seem to be no good moves is crucial. When things get unbearably difficult and the struggle begins there are a few things you can try. First, do not put it on only your shoulders. You should share every burden that you can with the maximum number of brains. Businesses, especially technology businesses, are extremely complex. Do not take the struggle personally; evaluating yourself does not help the situation. Do not be too positive. Accentuating the positive and ignoring the negative is fruitless. Most of the time, employees already know what the negative is, so this makes you seem dishonest. It is a much better idea to give the problem to the people who might be able to fix it. Transparency about your company's problem is important for three key reasons. The first reason is trust, and without it, communication breaks down. The second is that the more brains working on the hard problems, the better. The third reason is that bad news travels fast and good news travels slowly. A company culture that discourages the spread of bad news often allows that news to lie dormant until the company fails.

You will probably have to lay people off at some point. First, get your head right by focusing on the future of the company rather than the past.

Do not delay. If word leaks out before you execute the decision, a whole new set of issues will arise. Be clear about why you are laying people off. If it is because the company failed to hit its plan, then admit company failure. Train your managers to handle their own department layoffs. They should be clear that the decision is non-negotiable. Be prepared with details about benefits and support the company will provide. After laying people off, it is important to address the entire company. Be visible and be present.

Another challenge will be firing executives. The first step is to figure out what was wrong with the hiring process. Did you do a poor job defining the position? Did you hire for a lack of weakness rather than for strengths? Many times venture capitalists hire someone "bigger" than they need. You should only hire people who can run a large-scale organization if you have one, not if you hope to have one someday. Did the executive have the wrong kind of ambition? Ambition for the company is much different than ambition for oneself. Did you fail to integrate the executive?

Once you have decided to fire an executive, there are three goals you should have for informing the board: Get their support and understanding, get their input and approval for the separation package, preserve the reputation of the fired executive. When the time comes to speak with the executive there are three keys to doing so: Be clear about the reasons, use decisive language, and have the severance package ready.

Key Takeaways

- Don't shoulder company problems on your own; share them with the people that might be able to help fix them.
- Think about where the hiring process went wrong when you determine that you need to fire an executive.
- Be transparent about reasons for layoffs.

5: Take Care of the People, The Products, and the Profits – in That Order

Taking care of the people that work for you is the hardest, but most important job you have. Don't just tell them what to do, but be sure to tell them why you want them to do it.

It is extremely important to invest in training. People are your most important asset and good training increases productivity, the ability of managers to monitor performance, and the quality of the product. People need to know what knowledge they need to do their jobs well. Functional training should be tailored to the specific job the employee will do. Management training is also essential. Managers need to know what your expectations are. Training needs to be mandatory. Teach management training yourself.

It is very important to remember that being a big company executive is very different from being a small company executive. Big company executives are driven by interruptions while startup executives know that nothing happens unless they make it happen. If you hire the wrong match for your company, two dangerous results can occur. If there is a rhythm mismatch your executive will wait for something to happen, and your employees will wonder what he does all day. With a skill set mismatch you may end up with an executive who is good at complex decision-making, prioritization, organizational design, process improvement, and organizational communication but has no skills in running a high-quality hiring process or creating a process from scratch. In order to avoid disaster when hiring executives, be sure to screen for mismatches during interviews.

Once the right people are on board, it is important to avoid being misinterpreted as a leader. Managers must realize that anything that is going to be measured creates certain employee behaviors. It is important to think carefully about what employee behaviors you are looking for, so that you don't create behaviors that are worse than the situation you are trying to manage. It is also important to avoid management debt. Management debt is when you make an expedient, short-term management decision with an expensive, long-term consequence. It is also important to have a great HR department. A great human resources manager will have world-class process design skills, be a true diplomat, have great industry knowledge, and have the intellect to be the CEO's advisor.

Key Takeaways

- High quality training is the most important investment you can make.
- A great human resources department is crucial for running your business well.

- A big company executive has a very different role than a small company executive.

6: Concerning the Going Concern

As a company grows, it changes. It is important to minimize politics within your organization. One of the biggest issues behind politics is when people advance their careers or their agendas because of something besides merit or contribution. In order to avoid promoting politics within your company, you will need to build strict processes for organizational design, performance evaluations, promotions, and compensation. It is okay to use titles as long as you have a highly disciplined and properly constructed promotion process. If you don't have this in place, your employees will become obsessed with inequalities.

Sometimes, smart people can be bad employees. Intelligence is one important characteristic for any employee to have, but it should be accompanied by reliability, the ability to work hard, and the ability to work well with others.

Bringing in experienced people at the right time is key to your company's speed of growth and success rate. Experienced employees can come with some challenges, however. They often come with their own culture, they know how to work the system, and they know that you do not know how to do what they do. It is important to measure the success of experienced employees by measuring results against objectives, management skills, innovation, and their ability to work well with others.

One-on-one meetings between employees and managers are an important part of a well-designed communication architecture. They are a place for employees to discuss brilliant ideas, pressing issues, and chronic frustrations.

It is important to decide what will be most important in your culture. Establishing core values that drive your business will help your organization achieve its goals, preserve its key values, and become a better place to work.

As the company grows, communication, common knowledge, and decision-making all become more difficult. To scale appropriately, find an experienced mentor. As your business grows, you will need to specialize and the need for a strong organizational design will become crucial. First, you'll need to decide what needs to be communicated and what needs to be decided, and then you'll need to prioritize the most important communication and decision paths. Finally, you'll need to decide who will run these groups and identify any cross-organizational challenges. Focus on output first. How will you know if you are getting what you want?

Key Takeaways

- Smart people can be bad employees.
- Determine what you'd like your company culture to be, then model and promote it.
- Find an experienced mentor to guide you as your company grows.

7: How to Lead Even When You Don't Know Where You Are

As the CEO of a startup, it is crucial to focus on what needs to be right rather than worrying about what is wrong. One of the most difficult challenges is keeping your mind in check. You need to be able to move aggressively and decisively without acting insane. To calm your nerves, find someone you can talk to that understands what you're going through, put your ideas, challenges, and fears on paper, and focus on where you are going, not what you are trying to avoid. Great leaders can articulate the company vision, have the right kind of ambition, can get people to achieve the vision, and have skills for peacetime and wartime. One of the key skills of a great leader is giving feedback. Effective feedback comes from the right place, is authentic, and is direct, but not mean. Feedback should be a dialogue rather than a monologue.

Key Takeaways

- Keep your mind in check.
- Focus on where you want to go rather than what you want to avoid.
- Give timely, effective feedback.

8: First Rule of Entrepreneurship: There Are No Rules

There are no rules in business. Things may seem to be going well, but they can change in an instant. You need accountability and creativity to succeed in business. Accountability is key for many things including effort, promises, and results. How you should hold someone accountable for their results depends upon their seniority, the difficulty of the project they are held accountable for, and the amount of risk. More specifically, senior employees should be able to forecast their results more accurately than new employees. If their project is difficult, or if it is hard to make an accurate prediction, maybe they should not be held as accountable. Finally, not all risks are good risks. Only punish the risks that have a poor outlook for a reward. Hold your employees to a high standard. Executives must keep up with how the business changes. Warn them that if they can not keep up, even if they are doing a good job, you will have to fire them.

Companies sell for several reasons. If you are early on in a large market and you have a good chance of becoming number one in that market it is a good idea to remain a stand-alone company. If you determine that you need to sell, mute your emotions and be transparent with employees and stakeholders.

Key Takeaways

- There are no rules in entrepreneurship.
- Creativity is an essential skill in starting and running your business.
- If you have the opportunity to become number one in your market, remain a stand-alone company.

9: The End of the Beginning

After selling Opsware, Ben worked for Hewlett-Packard, but he knew he wanted to do something else. He decided that he wanted to start a venture capital firm. He wanted to create a firm that was specifically designed to help technical founders run their own companies. There are two deficits that a founder CEO has when compared with a professional CEO: the skill set and the network.

While his firm could not give a founder CEO all the skills he or she needed, they could give them mentorship. Therefore, all of their partners had to be effective mentors for a founder CEO. Then they decided to find the network. Applying CAA's operating model to venture capital, they built networks of large companies, executives, engineers, press and analysts, investors and acquirers. While doing all this, Ben was not considered a good CEO, but he is now. He has learned that the hard things will always be hard, but it has been worth it to work through them to fulfill his dreams.

Key Takeaways

- The best entrepreneurs work with the best venture capital firms.
- It is impossible to give a founder CEO all of the skills he will need, but it is possible to be a good mentor.

- The hard things in business will always be hard, but with courage and determination, success can be yours.

A Reader's Perspective

In *The Hard Thing About Hard Things: Building a Business When There Are No Easy Answers*, Ben Horowitz tells personal stories about his challenges and successes starting and running everything from a technology start-up to a highly respected venture capital firm. Based in part on his popular blog, Ben uses a no-nonsense approach to give practical business management advice to his readers complete with profanity and rap lyrics to make it not only an informational read, but also an entertaining one at times. A well-respected entrepreneur, Ben tells it like it is and infuses humor into his story and chunks of advice to soften the frequent blows about how difficult the process can be. Though the theme of the book seems to be that anyone can do what Ben has done as long as they are strong and courageous, many parts of the book were so focused on the "hard things" that the reader wonders why anyone would want to.

The beginning of the book reads like a memoir, with Ben detailing his lessons learned from a childhood dare, interactions with a high school basketball coach, and a blind date with a young woman who later turns out to be his wife. As he begins to share the experiences at the beginning of his career, the personal stories fade away and are replaced by stories of his tumultuous rise to success as an entrepreneur. With clever chapter titles and subtitles, Ben takes the reader with him on a roller-coaster ride of trials and successes in the world of technology-based business. Aside from a few brief mentions of his family and wife after the first chapter, he focuses only on his experiences with colleagues, competitors, and employees, almost as if the structure of the book sadly symbolizes a shift in the priorities in his life. Chapters one through three truly detail every step and misstep of Ben's journey early on in his career, some of which you would have to already be the CEO of a corporation to completely understand. Chapters four through eight focus on what he learned from the experiences in the book and include a few new stories of his adventures running subsequent companies, Loudcloud and Opsware. This section of the book got a bit repetitive when he recapped personal experiences, but offered some very practical advice about successfully running every part of a business. Finally, chapter nine focuses on his current venture as co-founder of Andreessen Horowitz, a capital venture company.

Even with the rap lyrics starting each new chapter and the profanity-laced titles for some of the strategies , this is more of an informational, self-help book for those in business than an entertaining read. This book might be best used as a reference, pulled from the shelf for practical advice on a relevant topic found in the table of contents. It certainly reads more like a business manual than a non-fiction book meant to be read from start to finish for entertainment.

Thank you for purchasing this summary. We hope you enjoyed it. If so, please leave a review.

We are also interested in talking to you to learn how we can improve! Please email instaread.summaries@gmail.com to take a quick survey. We will send you a $5 gift card from the store of your choice upon completion of the survey! -:)

Made in the USA
Lexington, KY
19 April 2014